Ira Beryl Brukner

Questions, Short Poems, Water & Air

Junction Press•San Diego•1998

Some of these poems have appeared in limited editions published by Konglomerati Press, Duck Press, and Inkling Press, and in the periodicals *Gierik*, *Gandhabba*, and *The Greenfield Review*.

Cover art by Hendriekus Vanderlee, courtesy of Kestrel Fine Arts. Photograph of Ira Beryl Brukner by Lee A. Melen.

Library of Congress Catalogue Number: 98-065855
ISBN: 1-881523-08-X
Junction Press PO Box 40537 San Diego CA 92164

for Jill and Raphael

Contents

Questions

are you happy

is there plutonium in your lung

can your neighbors read and write

is race a myth

are you graceful like an elm

is your stomach distended from hunger

are there rouge dabs in the sky

what is the taste of gold

are you a stranger in your homeland

do your vows harm others

can you propagate light through space

how brief is nirvana

is the sea-bottom constantly rising

is your consciousness unemployed

can you hurry love

were you born in a bunker

is number unity

is there architecture in a wave

are you in exile from alicnation

have you groped through heavy smoke

which rivers have you crossed

is revolution your daily bread

have you stopped taking leaps of faith

what can we do about rape

do you live from crisis to crisis

have you incited a riot

who needs your advice

what do you see in a grain of sand

are you falling in love

is war inevitable

is the moon howling at you

for whom is the swastika horrific

was the hypotenuse discovered on the harp

do your ribs rotate as you breathe

why do you survive

are you meditating in a mudslide

is there nuance in your ecstasy

can you heal yourself

have you drawn water from a well

are you unafraid of death

are you armored against affection

which secrets have you divulged

what is nothing

have you bathed in the light

do absences crowd you

have you watched dust under stress

are you dancing with yourself

when is the festival of laughter

can you quantify the unobserved

who depends upon you

have you fibrillated on a footpath

were you promiscuous on an isthmus

was your hand cut off for stealing

does one mask lead to another

can you conjure confidence

do you sing of disarmament

is there a plague nearby

were you quarantined

how old is the cure for cancer

is your energy delightful

what do you know to be true

are you immune to toxic shock

is your conscience fiction

what modes do you perceive

why be curious

can you get satisfaction guaranteed

what is mere anarchy

did you inherit a munitions factory

are collapsed alveoli ventilated by yawning

are minute particles kinetic in a gas

have you seen a volcano spew a plume of ash

who chopped down the yew groves

were you nervous on the verge of virginity

is your verse polymorphous

are you classless

were you in combat

what have you accomplished

are you crawling from bed to desk and back

is emptiness your territory

is the military invading your mind

is humanity descended from a coral-stem

are there bars on your windows

can enmity be ended by friendliness

can I get a witness

have you tried a little tenderness

are you an eccentric observer on a rotating disc

do you refrain from vengeance

which plumage are you in

can you perceive yourself in the act of perception

how much is wool worth

would you bombard an electron

what has value greater than itself

is there enough common wealth

do you contemplate sky

did you cry for a vision on a mountain

is the ivorybill woodpecker extinct

is most of your motion improvisation

what lies do you repeat

what is just

are you relentlessly anxious

is your depression intractable

have you got a pistol to your head

is the death-urge in you dead

is there a galaxy with bluer skies

do you believe in blessing

are you watching the night

is this an unguarded moment

do rents grow out of the soil

are you dedicated to desire

did you paint a couch in the middle of a jungle

has nicotine got a nail in you

have you wasted your life

do you genuflect

do you flinch at flattery

were you in a migrant-labor camp

what do you need to know

who underestimates your intelligence

is your aura epileptic

were you wild in the joy of thought

is the shape of your esophagus shifting

were you removed from your home

did you spend this morning crying

do you recognize yourself in others

do you forgive those who trespass against you

were you there when they were crucified

whose presidents smell like guns

are your priorities corporate

whose landlords smell like arson

have you abandoned hope

was the public instructed to ignore you

are you ashamed of your background

would you build a prison

are you learning how to listen

does argument strike you as absurd

are you too gone to wait and serve

is your wisdom compassionate

how long has the dragonfly been small

were you stymied by an award

are you rampant upon a plain of periwinkles

are you looking for a job

are you in a mad scramble for love

is it vitreous behind your eyeballs

are you in a diaphanous landscape

are you sifting thread through a sieve

were you disenfranchised by a parliament

are you an apprentice raising a tempest

is your library near a willow branch

were you denied medical treatment

who lugged the stones for the pyramids

is your potential immeasurable

is your emancipation imminent

why do chromosomes spindle

do you refuse to serve in the armed forces

is impatience a familiar trait

do you have trouble concentrating

have you felt thought

is there a sea-horse in your brain

do you share your knowledge

do you dance standing on your head

have you found a newt fossil yet

is all the joy within you gone

is there an electric-chair on your charm bracelet

are you walking through the shadows of bare branches

did your pressure just drop

has your wig turned gray

is there a contraction in the direction of your motion

was your first step an idea

what do you remember from your childhood

is the fat of the striped bass polluted

are you mourning a loss

how long will you be in this quadrant

with whom do you feel solidarity

are you holding on to truth

are your knees deep in cashmere mist

will you rebel against death

what is the code of the west

are you an optimist

were you awakened by a whippoorwill

have you been to a slaughterhouse

who loves you

what have you given away

has loneliness left you alone

were you in jail

is there water on the moon

have you seen the desert ablaze

where does it hurt

do you oppose nuclear explosion

what are you thinking

how did music begin

is privacy a luxury

have you comforted the sick

were you brainwashed in school

are you tired of trees

how do you live

what are you seeking

is integrity obsolete

who do you love

must everything change

are you between laughter and song

has reason bocome unreason and right wrong

is there peace in outer space

which illusions have you dismissed

are you courageous

whose memories have you been

are you a jazz messenger

why a veil

is an idea no thing

how do you distinguish good from evil

can you shout the ineffable

what deals have you made with your dreams

Short Poems

summer

naked on the beach
nothing in mind
here comes a cloud

spring the birds

the air is full of cool water
we hike through the woods
son of a secretary and an upholsterer
daughter of a chemist and a nurse

I call them tree-clouds
those crab-apple blossoms
hovering in front of us
she calls them pillow-stuffing on a stick

green mountains

in the moon when blackflies bite
we build a smoke fire
and it rains hard

rotting logs
line the muddy trail

one tree's roots
like a wishbone
arch over green rock

and fiddleheads taste
like bean sprouts
and wood sorrel
like loquat

miles away
there is a pine ridge
we will camp in tonight

special delivery

our love our new-born baby
has a dimple in his right cheek
and the longest brown eyelashes
part polliwog-hummingbird
going from breast to breast
with kisses all over his inches
those little hands and feet
that rose-petal mouth moving
from a smile
to a scowl
in a heartbeat

two days old

bundled up
and snuggled against my chest
is our half-asleep boy

I walk through town
stopping now and then
to introduce him
to falling flowers of ice
and adults wowed by his nose

he cries and coos
massaging my ribs
with his pea-pod toes

zero

once upon a time
a woman made a mark in the sand
that was one straight line

she stared at her work
until the hot sun disappeared

the next day
she made many lines in the sand
then she moved to the shade
until the hot sun disappeared

that night she dreamt
that the ends of one line
curved towards each other
and rolled away

recapitulation

not enough air
not hot enough

forest in one
drop of water

out of the wave
on the mud-flat

lung-fish leap-frog
flown snakes flower

and then the embryo
heart four chambers
becomes more monkey

under the yellow-leaf tree
in the white morning-light
I run jump jump all around

lullaby

in the bay of rainbows
near the sea of clouds
cows fly over the valley
wind elopes with the roof

on tour with Jill

after miles of modern dance
she crawls into bed
and I welcome her
into my arms

she rubs the sandpaper bottoms
of her feet together
like a bug before rainclouds
and heads for the underside of a leaf

presto sand
deep drift

what a woman
I am wide awake

Raphael

rubbing my calf
with his head
under the desk

rubbing my head
with his calf
under the desk

rocking his rocker
after standing on his horse

our wedding day

past morning glories by tiger lilies
black birds curve around a blue lake

wind blows willow split second fire
grumbling thunder booming down rain

cruelty

man beats man with baseball
bat against the arm the arm

hurt man begins to fall down
I yell at the top of my lung

the crowd stares at me
bat-man backs off done

somebody call an ambulance
line too long at pay-phone

almost fifty-three

dead one day
bye bye belt
carried too big chair
up three flight stair

daddy draft dodger caught
malaria during war worlds
was tender and bald
kissing mama in the hall

we took great showers together
he sang opera in bed

to whom it may concern

are you talking with the birds now
full moon all night long
are you wrestling with your shadow
turning circles for a song

in the park

swinging on the swings
higher and higher
my toes touch the sky

two girls do it
one standing up
one sitting down
and a girl on the ground
screaming screaming all of us now

untitled

a waterfall in my head
life without dread
no confidence in delusion
wretchedness unbiting
breath unheld

between the feathers of a wing
sunshine predicted

at night this strange sound
like bulls running through town

Water

a.

great lake
robin's-egg blue
speed boat waves
shall we canoe

walk that talk
get on down
roll that rock
up with sound

endlessnesses
pants to match the map

olives and grapes
leaves and vines
goat bells horse bells

start again
spring cometh in
jump to it

and then they made love
warm bodies
cool wind

half moon silver
over afternoon green
underwater clouds

drops of liquid
from the falling sky

hooray for lilac
and whiffs of alfalfa
aphids in the floor plans
petunias near the steps

b.

speeding and stopping like
horizontal exclamation points
disguised as squirrels
across green grass

below the hollow
listening to my heart
kite tail gaggles of geese
blowing through the white

a high-flying kiwi
is playing the piano
I forget my slow foot
and jump on the table

trumpet charms
a sitting woman
she shimmies up quick
on strong legs

drummer drifts
bass is on the phone
a light rain falling
we walk-skip home

dancing upside-down
lightning free
dancing inside-out
touch me

calla lily
near the straw hat
of a gardener

brush of air
through the trees

c.

pin-thin woman in high heel
street hot street flat wok
who off drops down no sound
street hot street flat wok

soft night
cool canal
gold shimmering
in ripples of light

hawk over head
dive dive dive
horses running
butterfly leaf

brown round bales of hay
like wheels of tumbleweed

a full moon
milks heat from flesh
and blots out sleep

claps fear
mouse fear
mouse claps fear

d.

he sang before he talked
he danced before he walked

I fell in love with her
the first time I saw her

names for rains
fire behind mist

shall I compare her to him
like apples and oranges then

on the roof
sun and wind

e.

save the fire
and the photographs

as for all of us
are we related

lions and tigers and bears
dream planet rock

east side west side
where a nickel costs a dime
uptown downtown
around the sunlight

here we go swim
here we go ride
with friends from afar
and there they go back

in the ocean
naked again
to be and not to be
time out eternity in

f.

the postman smelled him
three days dead
maggots in his head
the policeman threw up

after the explosion
she was carried out
a dusty body
limp arms and torn legs

the crowd surrounded him
bludgeoned to death
street blood-red
skull shattered

g.

on my knees
near the fragrances
in a garden
with the bees

music unfolding
through cloud-quilt
between the seconds
under a dogwood

diverse excellence
this golden age

h.

he dreams of trees
green and unlimited
fluid wind
pin-points of rain

cottonwood fluff
floats in the air

as he writes
each letter disappears

i.

midmorning end of summer
near a vineyard hill
a toddler points out
a red bear in a balloon

arm over arm
while fluttering her legs
a swimmer
tilts her head for breath

in the grape-ripe air
a lucky man
I enter
cold clear water

Air

one

I saw my father dead
on a long white table

after being told to
I kissed him

my mother let her finger
linger on the lips
of her husband

as we were leaving
she squeezed his toes

two

millions homeless
millions millionaires

he wrinkles
she irons

bloody border
imaginary line

sleep full of laughter
emotions linked by molecular code

three

he pulled me out of a pounding wave
I paddled to his hips and hugged him

he lifted me onto his shoulders
I wrapped myself around him

four

blood on the back
of a black bull

after sword plunge
blood out of mouth

five

ribbed cloud
shimmering leaf

thrilled by air
lost in the chant

first day
of almost spring

six

at the touch of a button
the coffin descended
into the earth

when it stopped
my mother wailed

I tried to hold on to her
and my sister

the undertaker placed
a green plastic carpet
over the grave

seven

snow falling
like a galaxy of white minnows

wind currents ahead
and heat-seeking feet
in pursuit of justice
for whose good

sitting on a brownstone stoop
across from the Flatiron Building
near two three-card-monte games
sipping matzohball soup

eight

walking again
scattering red leaves
in the cold wind

past the half-dead
in free foodlines
and pert rabbits at desks
in a shoestore window

then deep undergound
on a fast train

sky fire sky fire
anybody gotta light
sky fire sky fire
I walk through the night